Smart Kids
Science

W9-AHG-366

priddy books
big ideas for little people

Contents

Note to parents

The experiments in this book will introduce children to simple scientific concepts and prompt them to explore and question the world around them. Many of the experiments will surprise children and adults alike, so get ready to have fun together!

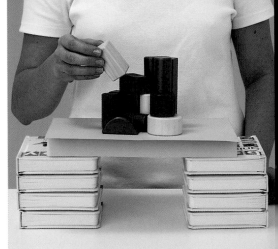

Agency photographs:
p.3 and p.35 middle right, Blair Seitz (Science Photo Library)
p.23 middle right, David Nunuk (Science Photo Library)
p.24 middle right, Damien Lovegrove (Science Photo Library)
p.46 bottom left, John Daniels (Ardea, London)
Additional photography on pages 2, 7, 17, 57 and 59 © Digital Vision

This edition copyright © 2010 St. Martin's Press, LLC
175 Fifth Avenue, New York, NY 10010.
Originally published as My Big Science Book copyright © 2003

Created for St. Martin's Press by
priddy books

Manufactured in China

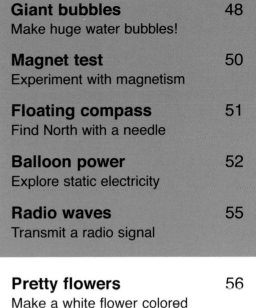

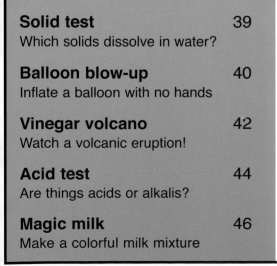
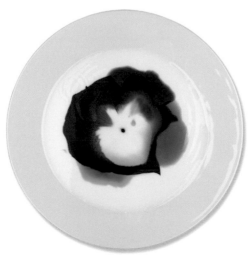

What you need

Starting your science lab

Getting started

All of the experiments in this book can be carried out with things you can find at home or in your local store. Many of the things you will need are shown on these pages, but check the 'You will need' section at the beginning of each experiment before you begin. Always ask before using anything at home!

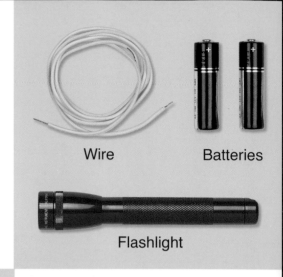

Wire

Batteries

Flashlight

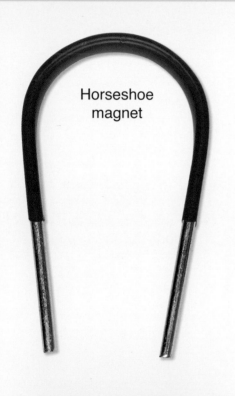

Horseshoe magnet

Bar magnet

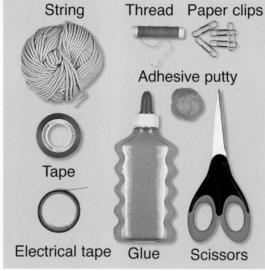

String

Thread

Paper clips

Adhesive putty

Tape

Electrical tape

Glue

Scissors

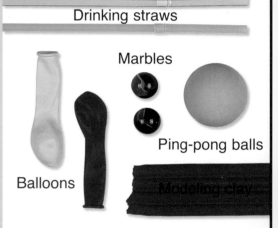

Drinking straws

Marbles

Ping-pong balls

Balloons

Modeling clay

Colored crayons

Paints

Paintbrushes

Colored pens

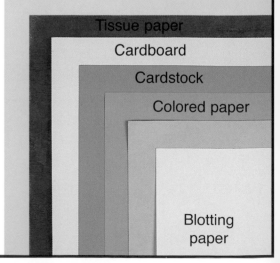

Tissue paper

Cardboard

Cardstock

Colored paper

Blotting paper

Different-sized plates and saucers

Glass bowls

Pitcher

Water

Milk

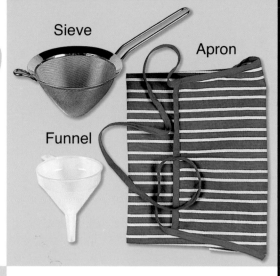

Sieve

Apron

Funnel

Metal spoons

Plastic spoons

Wooden spoon

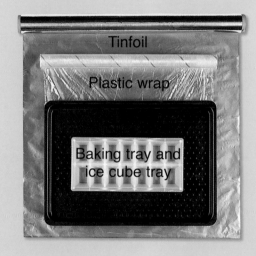

Tinfoil

Plastic wrap

Baking tray and ice cube tray

Mirror

Plastic soda bottles

Glass bottles

Glasses

Liquid soap

Cooking oil

Vinegar

Baking soda

Food coloring

Salt

Safe science

As a rule, ALWAYS ask an adult before doing any of the experiments. They will be able to help you find the things you need and help you out if necessary. Always clean up after you have finished, because some of the experiments are very messy. Most importantly, you should have lots of fun!

Rocket balloon

Make a balloon that flies like a rocket

You will need:

- piece of string (about 6 to 8 feet long)
- balloon
- 2 chairs
- drinking straw
- tape
- scissors

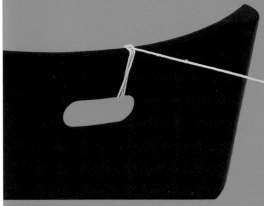

1 Tie one end of the string to the back of a chair.

2 Thread the straw onto the string and tie the other end of the string to the other chair.

3 Attach two pieces of tape to the straw as shown.

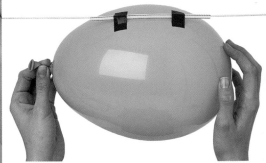

4 Inflate the balloon, hold the opening, and attach it to the straw with the tape.

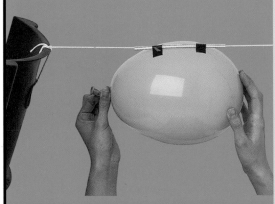

5 Pull the balloon to one end of the string and let go. What happens?

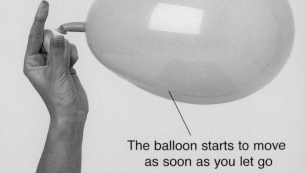

The balloon starts to move as soon as you let go

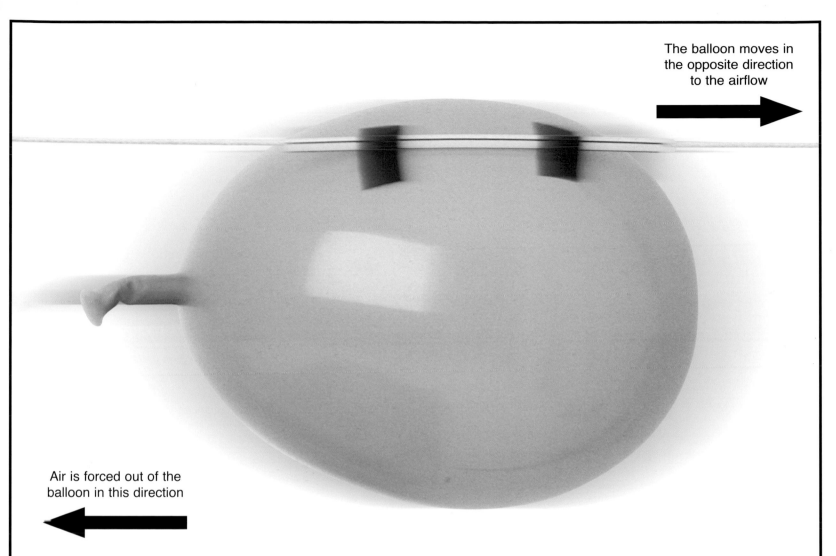

The balloon moves in the opposite direction to the airflow

Air is forced out of the balloon in this direction

Action and reaction

To make something move one way, a force has to work in the opposite direction – this is known as 'action and reaction.' The air inside the inflated balloon is pushing in all directions. When you let go of the balloon, air rushes out of the hole, creating a pushing force in the opposite direction. This makes the balloon move.

Rockets

Real rockets work in a similar way to your rocket balloon. A rocket engine works by exploding fuel inside a chamber that is open at the bottom. The force of the exploding fuel coming out of the rocket creates an opposite force that pushes the rocket up and on into space.

Bottle diver

Make your own deep sea diver

You will need:

- large plastic soda bottle
- water
- thick tinfoil
(a disposable food tray is ideal)
- flexible drinking straw
- adhesive putty
- glass
- paper clip
- scissors • pen

1 Trace or copy this picture of a diver onto a piece of foil.

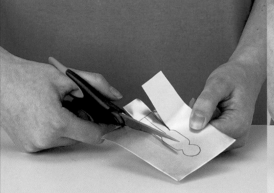

2 Carefully cut around the outline of the diver.

3 Cut off the flexible section of the straw, leaving about 1 inch of straw on either side.

4 Bend the straw, and push each end onto the paper clip.

5 Carefully slide the paper clip onto the diver as shown.

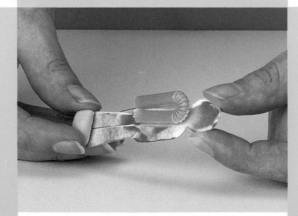

6 Stick a small piece of adhesive putty onto the diver's feet.

7 Place the diver in a glass of water to make sure it floats.

8 Fill the bottle with water right to the top. Put the diver in and screw the lid on tightly.

9 Squeeze the bottle. What happens? Can you make the diver float anywhere in the bottle?

Density and diving

The air inside the bent straw is less dense (packed together) than the water around it, making the diver float. Squeezing the bottle forces water into the straw, making it more dense inside and making the diver sink. When you stop squeezing, the water density in the straw decreases and the diver floats to the top.

Floating fish

Fish make themselves float and sink by breathing gases in and out of an organ called a swim bladder. Breathing in gas makes the fish less dense, so it floats. Breathing the gas out makes it sink.

Sky diver

Make a model parachute

You will need:

- piece of plastic sheeting about 16-inches square (a plastic bag is ideal)
- 4 x 12-inch pieces of thread
- modeling clay
- scissors
- paper clip

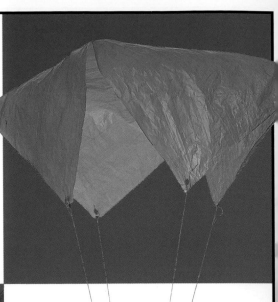

1 Cut a hole in each corner of the plastic sheeting. Attach a piece of thread to each corner.

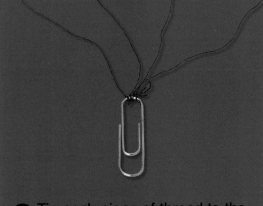

2 Tie each piece of thread to the paper clip. This is the 'harness' for your sky diver.

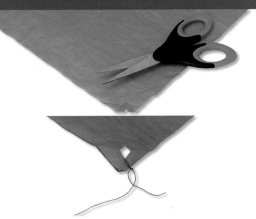

3 Make your sky diver out of a piece of modeling clay.

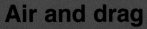

4 Press the paper clip into your sky diver. Fold the parachute and throw it as high as you can.

Air and drag

The parachute and sky diver are pulled to the ground by the force of gravity. As they fall, the air trapped beneath the parachute pushes up slightly, slowing down the parachute's fall. The force of the air pushing against the parachute is called air resistance, or drag.

Floating test

Why do some things float?

You will need:

- large bowl or sink
- water
- objects to test:
  solid and hollow things,
  objects made from
  different materials
- modeling clay

Float or sink?

Whether things float or sink depends upon their density – how tightly packed together the material inside them is. Metal ships are very heavy, but are big and hollow (not very dense). This is how they are able to float on the sea.

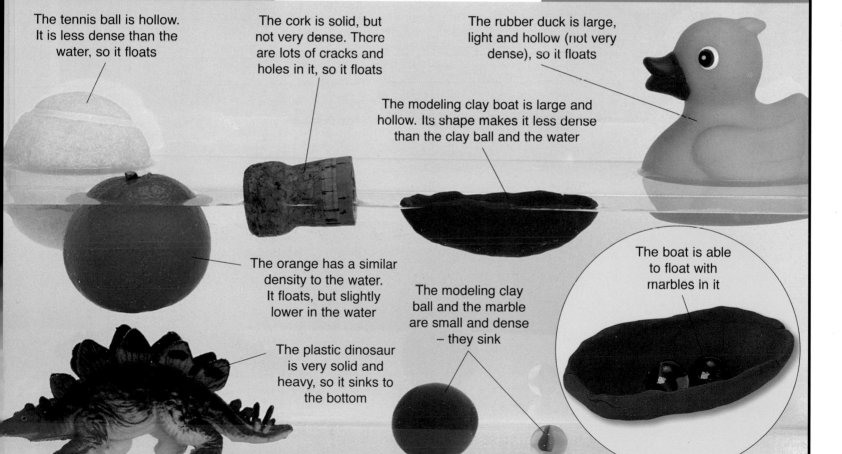

The tennis ball is hollow. It is less dense than the water, so it floats

The cork is solid, but not very dense. There are lots of cracks and holes in it, so it floats

The rubber duck is large, light and hollow (not very dense), so it floats

The modeling clay boat is large and hollow. Its shape makes it less dense than the clay ball and the water

The orange has a similar density to the water. It floats, but slightly lower in the water

The modeling clay ball and the marble are small and dense – they sink

The boat is able to float with marbles in it

The plastic dinosaur is very solid and heavy, so it sinks to the bottom

1 Test all your objects by dropping them in the water. Which ones float and which ones sink?

2 Make a ball out of the modeling clay – it will sink to the bottom. Mold it into a boat shape and see if you can make it float with something in it.

Paper airplane

Make an airplane that really flies

You will need:

- piece of 8½ x 11 inch paper
- paper clip

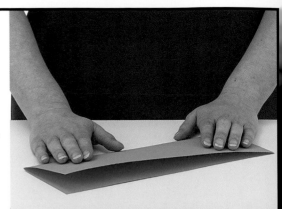

1 Fold the paper in half lengthwise. Make sure the fold is as straight as possible. Then unfold the paper.

2 Fold one corner in so that its edge meets the fold. Do the same with the opposite corner.

3 Fold the paper back along the first fold that you made.

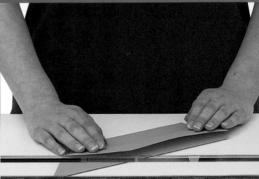

4 Fold one side down to meet the first fold. Turn it over and do the same on the other side.

5 Push a paper clip onto the nose of your airplane. Now your airplane is ready to fly.

Aerodynamics

The paper airplane flies through the air because of its pointed shape. This is called an aerodynamic design. As it cuts through the air, the air beneath its wings pushes the airplane up in the opposite direction to the force of gravity, which is pulling it to the ground.

Paper helicopter

Make a spinning, flying machine

You will need:

- piece of paper (about 8 inches x 6 inches)
- pen or pencil
- scissors
- paper clip

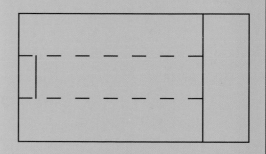

1 Carefully copy this pattern onto your piece of paper.

2 Cut along the two dotted lines as shown above.

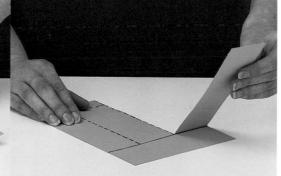

3 Fold one of the flaps along the solid black line.

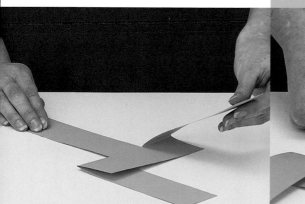

4 Turn the helicopter over and fold over the second flap.

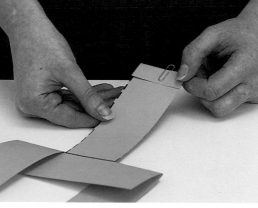

5 Fold over the small flap at the bottom, and slide on the paper clip. Throw it into the air as high as you can.

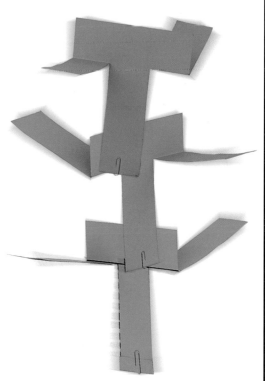

Spinning wings

As your paper helicopter falls, the air pushing against the wings makes them spin. The spinning wings have the effect of slowing the helicopter's fall to the ground.

13

Air action

How does air make things fly?

You will need:

- 2 ping-pong balls
- balloon
- hairdryer
- thread
- drinking straw
- scissors
- tape

Pressure points

The faster that air is moving, the lower its pressure. High-pressure air moves towards low-pressure air, and anything in-between will be pushed as well. Blowing between the ping-pong balls reduces the air pressure between them, so the high-pressure air on either side pushes them together.

1 Cut two pieces of thread, each about 10 inches long. Tape them to the ping-pong balls.

You could use a climbing frame or pole

2 Tie the threads to something, about 4 inches apart. Allow the balls to hang at the same height.

3 Hold the drinking straw about 4 inches behind the balls and blow between them.

4 The balls should move together. Why do you think that happens?

The ping-pong ball 'floats' in the airflow

The balloon floats higher than the ping-pong ball

The airflow keeps the balloon afloat, even at an angle

5 Point the hairdryer upward, switch it on and put a ping-pong ball in the airflow.

6 Now do the same with a balloon. What happens?

7 Try tilting the hairdryer to one side. Can you keep the balloon in the airflow?

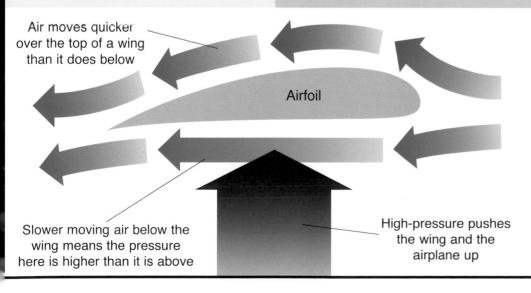

Air moves quicker over the top of a wing than it does below

Airfoil

Slower moving air below the wing means the pressure here is higher than it is above

High-pressure pushes the wing and the airplane up

Floating and flying

The air moving upward hits the bottom of the ball or balloon and slows down, which creates an area of higher pressure. The high-pressure air pushes up against gravity, which is pulling the ball or balloon down. This effect is used in airplane wings to make them fly. The curved shape of a wing is called an airfoil.

15

Bridge shapes

Find out how bridges stay up

You will need:

- 6 pieces of 8½ x 11 inch cardstock
- 8 books of the same size
- tape
- objects to test the strength of the bridges

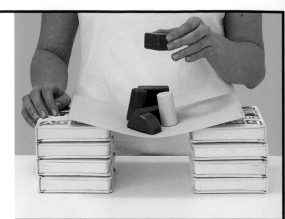

1 Put a piece of cardstock across two piles of books. How much weight will the bridge hold?

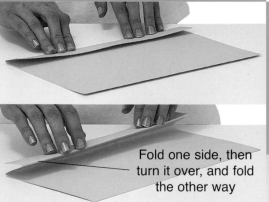

Fold one side, then turn it over, and fold the other way

2 Fold a second piece of cardstock lengthwise into a zigzag shape as shown.

3 Place the zigzag shape across the books. Then place another piece of cardstock on top.

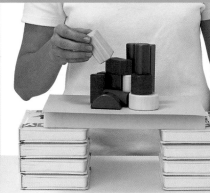

4 Put some weights on top of the bridge. Does it hold more or less weight than the first bridge?

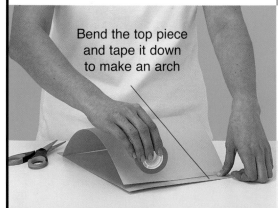

Bend the top piece and tape it down to make an arch

5 Place one piece of cardstock on top of the other, about 1 inch from the end. Tape it down.

Complete the bridge by placing a piece of cardstock on top

6 Place the ends of the arch on top of half of the books. Place the remaining books on top to hold it.

7 Put some weights on top of your arch bridge. How much weight does it hold?

The bridge is only supported at the sides, so the weight pushes it down in the middle

Balanced forces

Bridges support their own weight as well as the things that go across them. They do this by spreading the force of the weight through the bridge. The bridge structure 'pushes' against the force and the weight is supported. These are called balanced forces.

Strong triangles

The triangular shapes in this suspension bridge are keeping the forces balanced.

The triangular shapes in the zigzag section spread the force of the weight across the bridge

Arch bridges

Arch shapes are often used to provide strength in bridges and other structures.

The arch shape spreads the force of the weight to the books

Balancing act

Make an acrobatic clown

You will need:

- piece of paper
- colored markers
- 2 small coins
- glue
- scissors
- drinking straw or pencil

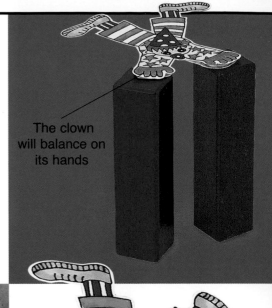

The clown will balance on its hands

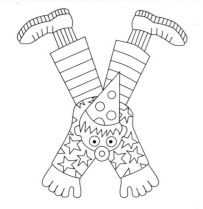

1 Make two copies of this picture on a piece of white paper.

2 Cut out both of the clown shapes and color them in.

Balance the clown on its nose on the end of a straw, pencil, or finger

3 Place one shape face down on a table. Cover it with glue and place the coins on the clown's hands.

4 Place the other shape on top (colored side up). Line up the edges and leave it to dry.

Balancing act

The coins placed between the clown's hands have shifted the center of gravity – the point where the weight is focused. As long as the center of gravity is over an object, the clown will remain balanced and will not fall off.

Seeing sound

How does sound make movement?

You will need:

- bowl
- plastic wrap
- rice
- metal tray
- metal spoon

Visual vibrations

Hitting the tray with the spoon makes the air around it vibrate (move around very quickly). The air travels in waves in all directions. When the sound waves reach the plastic wrap, they make it vibrate, which makes the rice move. Our ears pick up sounds in this way.

1 Stretch a piece of plastic wrap tightly over the bowl.

2 Scatter some grains of rice across the top of the plastic wrap.

3 Hold the metal tray close to the bowl. Strike the tray with the spoon to make a loud noise. What happens to the rice?

Phone a friend

Make a string telephone

You will need:

- 2 strong paper cups
- piece of string (at least 12 feet long)
- scissors
- sharp pencil
- a friend

String vibrations

Sound waves travel through solid objects better than they do through the air. Speaking into a cup makes it vibrate, which makes the string vibrate in turn. The vibrations travel along the string to the other cup, which vibrates and reproduces the sound.

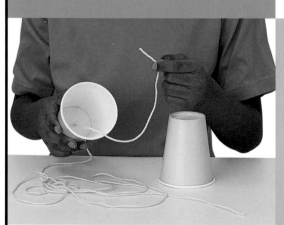

1 Use a sharp pencil to make holes in the bottom of the cups. Push the string through each hole.

2 Tie a knot in each end of the string inside the cups. The knots must be bigger than the holes.

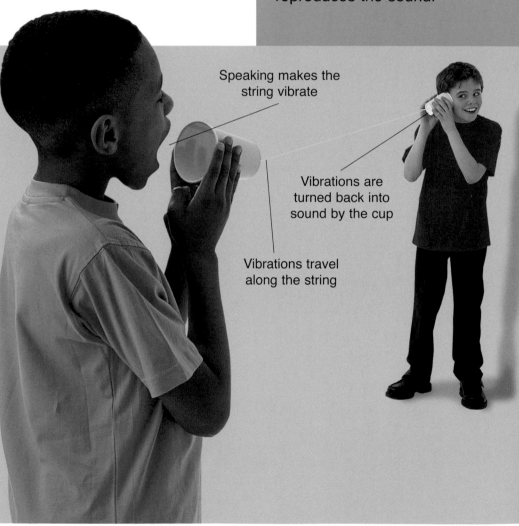

Speaking makes the string vibrate

Vibrations are turned back into sound by the cup

Vibrations travel along the string

3 Ask a friend to take one cup and move far enough away to make the string tight. One of you should speak into a cup, while the other holds their cup to their ear. Take turns speaking to one another.

Singing glass

Make a noise with a glass

You will need:

- glass with a long stem
- water

Good vibrations

The glass 'sings' because it is being made to vibrate by your moving finger. The sound you hear depends on the size and shape of the glass, and how much water is in it. A big glass filled with water will make a low note. A small glass with a little water will make a high note.

1 Half fill the glass with water. Dip your forefinger in it.

2 Hold the base of the glass firmly with one hand. Press down on the rim of the glass with your wet finger.

3 Slowly and steadily move your finger around the rim of the glass. It may take some practice, but you should be able to make a ringing sound come from the glass.

Bottle xylophone

Make music with bottles

You will need:

- 6 glass bottles
- wooden spoon
- water
- food coloring
- pitcher

Water music

Hitting the bottles with the spoon makes them vibrate and produce a sound. The more the bottle vibrates, the higher the note will be. The more water there is in a bottle, the less it vibrates, so less water means higher notes.

1 Fill one bottle with water, then fill each other bottle with slightly less than the bottle next to it.

2 Add some food coloring to help you see the different levels of water.

The less water there is in a bottle, the higher the note it will make

Tap each bottle with the spoon

3 Tap the bottles with the end of a wooden spoon. Can you play a tune?

Looking at light

How does light behave?

You will need:

- flashlight
- mirror
- piece of white paper

1 In a dark room, shine your flashlight at the wall. What happens if you move your flashlight?

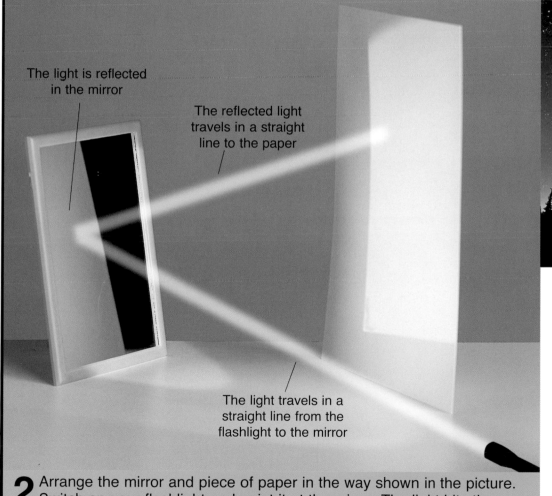

The light is reflected in the mirror

The reflected light travels in a straight line to the paper

The light travels in a straight line from the flashlight to the mirror

2 Arrange the mirror and piece of paper in the way shown in the picture. Switch on your flashlight and point it at the mirror. The light hits the shiny surface of the mirror and is reflected at an angle to the paper.

Light lines

Light travels in a straight line until it hits an object. It also travels faster than anything else – about 186,000 miles a second. The stars that you see at night are so far away that the light has taken many years to reach Earth, where we can see them.

Bending light

See how light can bend

You will need:

- glass
- water
- colored marker

Refraction

The pen looks bent at the point where it enters the water. This is because the light is being slowed down as it passes through the water. The image of the pen at that point takes longer to reach our eyes. This effect is called refraction.

The marker looks straight

The marker looks like it has a bend in it

1 Put the marker in the glass as shown. It should look as normal.

2 Now fill the glass with water, almost to the top. Does the marker look any different?

Mirages

Refraction happens in air when there is a difference in temperature. In deserts, light travels quicker through the hot air near the ground than it does through the cooler air above it. This makes things look closer than they actually are, or it can look like there is a lake up ahead. This illusion is called a mirage.

Mirror writing

Trick your eyes and brain

You will need:

- mirror with stand
- books
- paper
- pen or pencil
- large piece of cardboard

1 Make two piles of books of the same height. Put the piece of paper between the books.

2 Prop up the mirror behind the paper as shown.

Reverse writing

Our eyes and brain are used to seeing the words written normally, so seeing them written backwards makes it difficult to recognize and write even simple things, such as your name.

The mirror reflects your writing in the opposite direction, so everything appears backwards

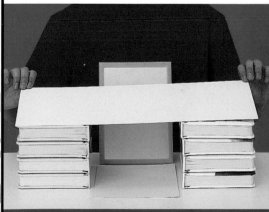

3 Put the large piece of cardboard across the top of the books as shown above.

4 Position yourself so that you can only see the paper in the mirror. Try writing your name when you look in the mirror. Do you find it easy to write?

Shadow puppets

Play with light to make shadows

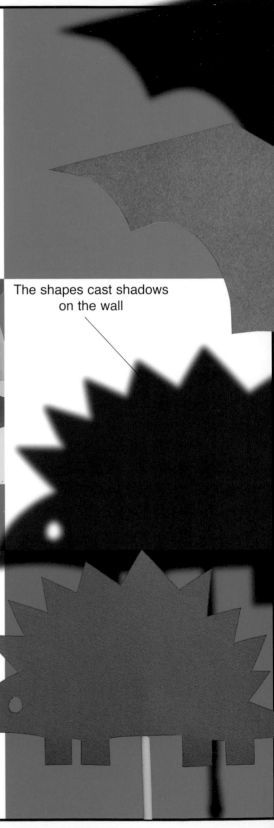

The shapes cast shadows on the wall

1 Draw some shapes onto the cardstock, or you could copy the shapes on these pages.

2 Carefully cut out the shapes.

3 Use tape to attach a drinking straw to one side of each of the shapes.

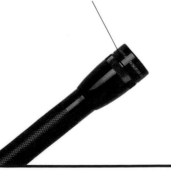

In a darkened room, hold the shapes against a wall, and shine your flashlight at them

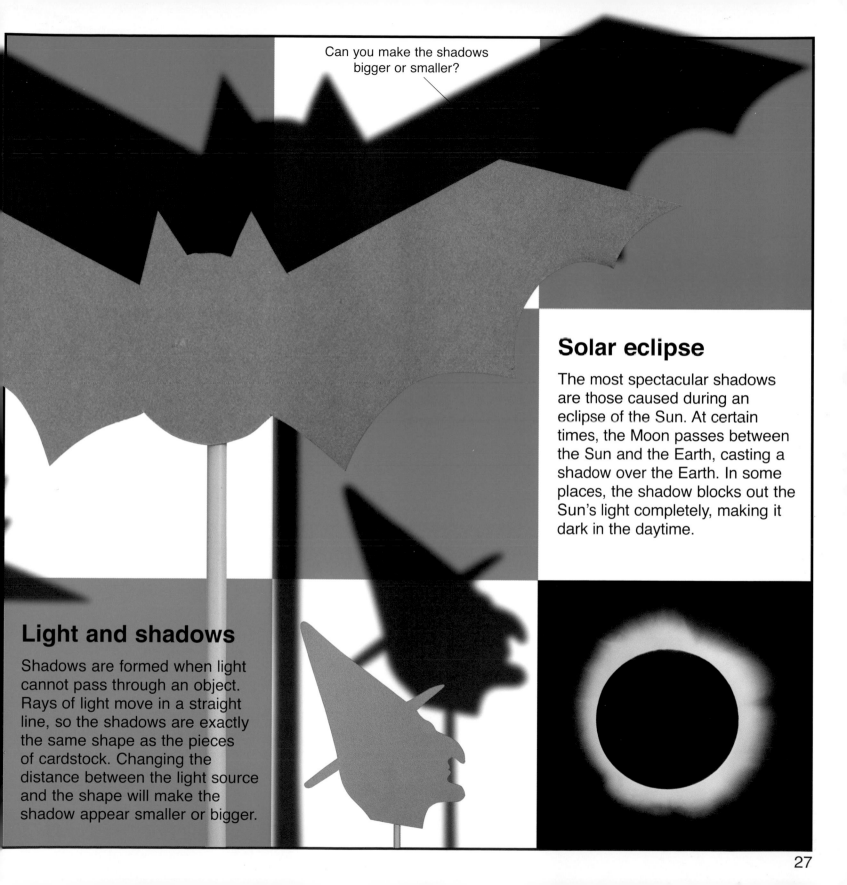

Can you make the shadows bigger or smaller?

Solar eclipse

The most spectacular shadows are those caused during an eclipse of the Sun. At certain times, the Moon passes between the Sun and the Earth, casting a shadow over the Earth. In some places, the shadow blocks out the Sun's light completely, making it dark in the daytime.

Light and shadows

Shadows are formed when light cannot pass through an object. Rays of light move in a straight line, so the shadows are exactly the same shape as the pieces of cardstock. Changing the distance between the light source and the shape will make the shadow appear smaller or bigger.

Optical illusions

Play tricks with your eyes

Seeing sense

You will not believe your eyes when you look at the pictures and patterns on these pages. These optical illusions work by arranging shapes in ways that fool your eyes and brain. You might see things that are not there, twisted shapes and even moving objects. Have fun, but staring at them for too long could make your eyes hurt!

Seeing the invisible

1 Can you see the two diamond shapes? Can you see an outline?

2 You can see a triangle, but where is its outline?

3 Look at the points where the lines meet. Do you see circles?

1

2

3

Moving circles

4 Stare at the center of the circles, and move your head backwards and forwards. Do the circles appear to move?

5 Stare at the center of the spiral spokes. Hold the page upright, and slowly twist it up and down. Do the spokes appear to twist and move?

4

5

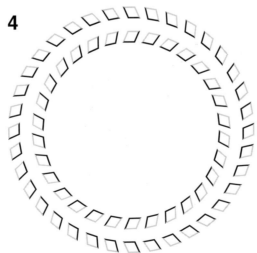
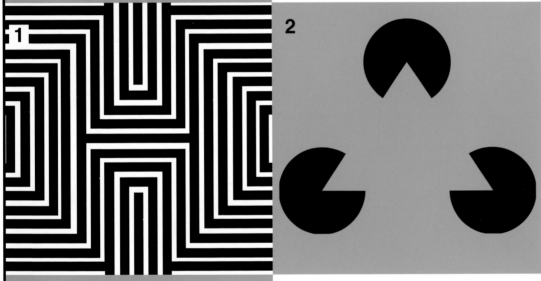
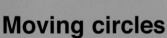
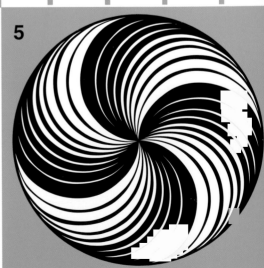

Straight lines?

6 The gray horizontal lines look like they slope. They are, in fact, absolutely straight.

7 The circles make the edges of the square appear to bend. They are perfectly straight.

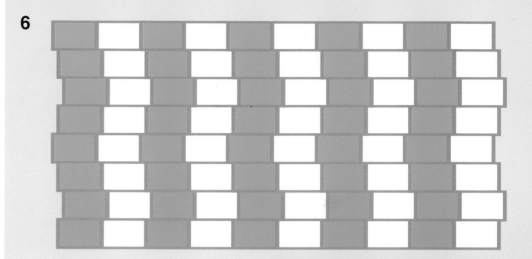

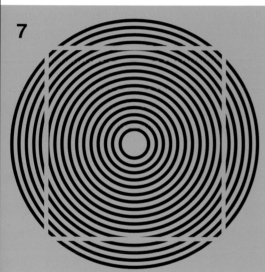

Flashing spots

8 Can you see gray spots flashing in the white circles? Can you touch one? Probably not – once you try to focus on one gray spot, it disappears.

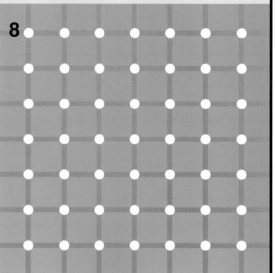

Two-in-one

9 What do you see? A rabbit or a duck?

10 Do you see a woman's face, or a man playing a saxophone?

More optical illusions

How are your eyes?

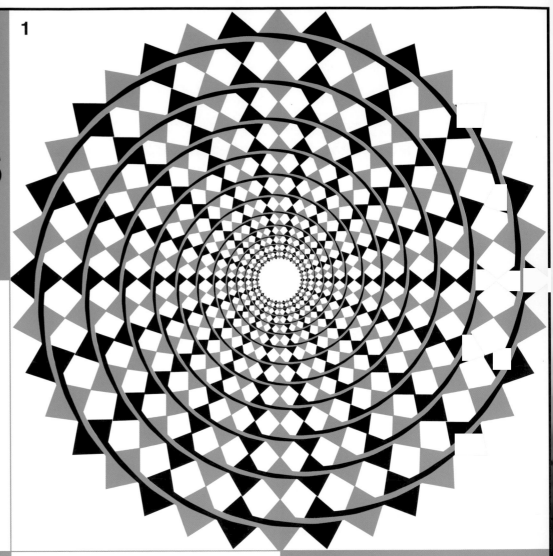

Spiral circles

1 At first glance, this illusion looks like a spiral. Take a closer look, and you will see that it is actually a series of circles. Follow them with your finger to check.

Big or small?

2 Which of the two black circles is the biggest? They are actually the same size.

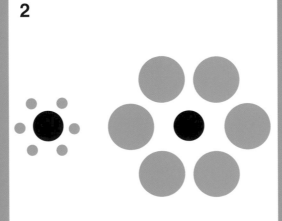

3 How about the two white lines? Is one longer than the other? Measure them with a ruler to find out.

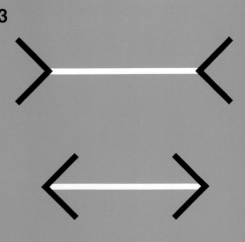

Picture mixer

Turn two pictures into one

You will need:

- 2 pieces of white paper
- pencil
- colored markers
- scissors
- glue

The bird appears to be in the cage

1 Copy each of these pictures onto two separate pieces of paper. Color in the bird.

2 Cut each picture into a circle about 3 inches across.

3 Lay one picture face down and cover it with glue. Put the pencil on it and stick on the other picture.

4 When the glue has dried, hold the pencil as shown. Rub your hands to make the picture spin.

Vision mix

We see the bird appear in the cage because the pictures are moving too quickly for our eyes and brain to tell the difference between the two. Cartoons and movies use this effect by moving a series of still pictures very quickly. This creates an illusion of movement.

Mixing colors

Mix paints to make new colors

You will need:

- paints: red, yellow, blue, white and black
- paintbrushes
- paper

1 Mix together red and yellow. What color does it make?

2 How about mixing yellow and blue? What do you get?

3 Now try blue and red. What color do they make?

4 Now try three colors – red, yellow and blue. What do these colors make?

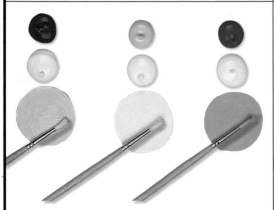

5 Try mixing some colors with white. Does it make the colors lighter or darker?

6 Now try mixing the same colors with black. What happens now?

Paints and pigments

The colors in paints and inks are produced by substances called pigments. Pigments absorb some colors and reflect their own. For example, red absorbs the colors green and blue and reflects red. Mixtures of different pigments create new colors by absorbing and reflecting different mixtures of color.

Color wheel

See spinning colors mix

You will need:

- white cardstock
- piece of string (about 4 feet long)
- sharp pencil
- scissors
- colored markers
- a friend

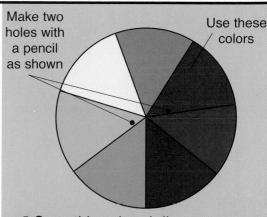

Make two holes with a pencil as shown

Use these colors

1 Copy this colored disc onto a piece of cardstock. Make it about 4 inches across.

2 Push the string through one hole and then back through the other.

3 Tie the two ends together and position the wheel halfway along the string.

4 Take hold of the string loop and pull it tight. Ask your friend to twist the wheel.

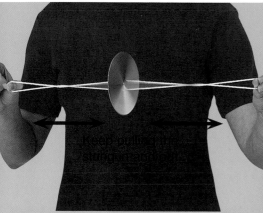

5 When your friend lets go of the wheel, pull the string in and out to keep the wheel turning.

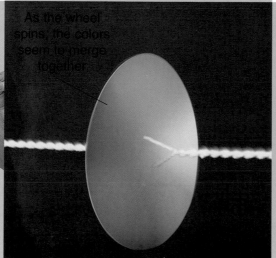

As the wheel spins, the colors seem to merge together

White colors

White light is made up of several different colors, a bit like the colors on your wheel. When you make the colors spin, they move too quickly for our eyes and brain to pick them out separately, so we see them as a blurred, grayish white color.

Pen colors

Discover the colors in pens

You will need:

- colored markers
- blotting paper
- scissors
- water
- teaspoon
- salt
- glass

1 Cut out a piece of blotting paper. It should be big enough to fit around the inside of the glass.

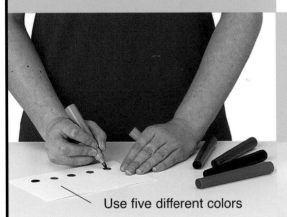

Use five different colors

2 Draw five colored ½-inch circles, about 1 to 2 inches from the bottom of the paper.

3 Pour water into the glass, until it is about ½-inch deep. Stir in a teaspoon of salt.

4 Roll the paper into a tube and put it in the glass. Leave it for about 30 minutes. What happens?

Candy colors

See the colors in candies

You will need:

- sugar-coated colored candies
- blotting paper
- scissors
- water
- small saucers

Move the candies around so that the color runs into the water

1 Pour a few drops of water into a saucer, and add four or five candies of the same color.

Colors before being soaked in water

Chromatography

The colors used in pens and candies are made up of several different substances called pigments. Different pigments move through the paper at different speeds, which shows the various shades that make up the colors. This is called chromatography. Scientists called chemists often use chromatography to identify different chemicals in substances.

Green splits into blue and yellow pigments

Dark colors such as black and brown contain the most pigments

The colors split as they are drawn up through the paper

The brown color contains blue pigment

2 Cut a strip of blotting paper and place one end in the colored water. Leave it to stand.

Orange contains some red pigment

Why not try some other colors?

Some colors, such as blue, contain only one pigment.

35

Changing states

Three experiments about solids, liquids and gases

You will need:

- water
- ice cube tray
- freezer
- food coloring
- pitcher
- plate
- saucepan lid
- boiling water
- plastic soda bottle

1 Fill an ice cube tray with water. Do not fill it to the top.

2 Add different colors of food coloring to the water. Leave the tray in the freezer overnight.

3 Take the tray out of the freezer. The water will have frozen into ice. Put the ice cubes on a plate.

4 As the ice warms up, it melts and changes back into water.

1 Ask an adult to fill a pitcher with boiling water. Hold a saucepan lid over it for about 20 seconds.

2 Take the lid away and look underneath. The steam has cooled and turned back into water.

Hot and cold

Water can be a solid, a liquid or a gas. A change in temperature can change it from one state to another. When it gets very cold, water freezes into solid ice, which melts back into a liquid when it gets warmer. Boiling water turns into a gas (steam) – this is called evaporation. As it cools, it returns to a liquid state. This is called condensation.

Fill the bottle right to the top

Water expands as it freezes, making the bottle bigger

Particle patterns

Solids, liquids and gases behave differently because of the way their particles are arranged. A solid's particles are tightly packed together, which makes its shape difficult to change. Liquid particles slide around, so a liquid takes the shape of its container. Gas particles move around very quickly and fill any space they are in.

Solid

Solid particles are arranged very close together

Liquid

Liquid particles stick to one another, but move around

Gas

Gas particles move away from each other very quickly

1 Fill a soda bottle with water and screw the lid on tightly. Leave it in the freezer overnight.

2 Take the bottle out of the freezer. What has happened?

Liquid mix

Do all liquids mix together?

You will need:

- glasses
- teaspoon
- water
- apple juice
- cooking oil
- liquid soap

Liquid mixtures

Apple juice and water are very similar liquids and mix together easily. Oil does not dissolve in water, but adding some liquid soap makes the droplets of oil mix into the water – at least for a while. This type of mixture is called an emulsion.

Apple juice

Cooking oil

Liquid soap

1 Pour some water into a glass. Add some apple juice and stir.

2 Pour water into a second glass. Next, pour in some cooking oil.

3 Add some liquid soap to the water and oil. Give it a stir.

Apple juice mixes easily with water – these are called miscible liquids

Water and oil do not mix together – they are called immiscible liquids

Liquid soap is an emulsifier – it makes the oil and water mix

Solid test

Which solids dissolve in water?

You will need:

- glasses
- hot and cold water
- teaspoon
- substances to dissolve – instant coffee, sugar, pudding mix, salt, sand, powder detergent

Dissolving solids

Try mixing various substances in glasses of hot and cold water. Salt, sugar, coffee and powder detergent are soluble – they will dissolve easily in water, especially if it is hot. Pudding mix contains dried egg, which starts to cook in hot water. Sand is insoluble – it will not dissolve in water, whether it is hot or cold.

Instant coffee
Cold   Hot

Sugar
Cold   Hot

Pudding mix
Cold   Hot

Salt
Cold   Hot

Sand
Cold   Hot

Powder detergent
Cold   Hot

Balloon blow-up

Inflate a balloon without touching it

You will need:

- small soda bottle
- balloon
- baking soda
- vinegar
- funnel
- teaspoon

1 Using a funnel, pour about a third of a cup of vinegar into the bottle.

2 Slide the balloon onto the funnel as shown here.

3 Put two teaspoons of baking soda into the balloon. Remove the funnel from the balloon.

4 Stretch the mouth of the balloon over the bottle, taking care not to let any of the baking soda drop into it. You might need an adult to help you with this.

5 Hold the bottle, lift up the balloon and empty the baking soda into the vinegar.

6 The baking soda and vinegar will foam in the bottle. What happens to the balloon?

Gas balloon

When the baking soda and vinegar mix together, they create a gas called carbon dioxide. All gases expand to fill any space available, so the carbon dioxide inflates the balloon.

The carbon dioxide gas produced by the baking soda and vinegar inflates the balloon

41

Vinegar volcano

Make a volcano erupt in your kitchen

You will need:

- 2 small plastic soda bottles
- large piece of cardstock
- scissors • tape
- pen or pencil
- vinegar • baking soda
- tablespoon • teaspoon
- food coloring
- liquid soap
- large plate or tray • funnel

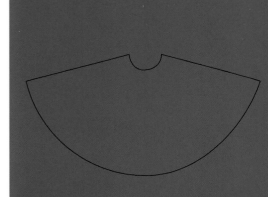

1 Copy the shape above onto the cardstock. It needs to be big enough to fit around a bottle.

2 Cut out the shape and bend it into a cone as shown. Secure it with tape.

3 Using a funnel, fill one of the bottles until it is about one-third full of vinegar.

4 Add a few drops of food coloring. We used red, but you can use any color.

5 Add one tablespoon of liquid soap, and put the bottle to one side.

6 Put the second bottle on a tray and add three teaspoons of baking soda.

7 Place the cone over the bottle. Make sure the hole is level with the bottle opening.

8 Using a funnel, pour in the vinegar and liquid soap mixture. Remove the funnel and wait...

Warning!

This experiment will make a mess – remember to clean up afterwards!

The mixture comes out of the bottle

Gases and bubbles

When the vinegar and baking soda mix together, they produce carbon dioxide gas. This gas creates bubbles in the vinegar and the liquid soap. The foaming, messy mixture expands and forces itself out of the top of the bottle.

The mixture oozes down the cone

Carbon dioxide gas forms bubbles in the mixture

Acid test

Are things acids or alkalis?

You will need:

- red cabbage
- 2 pitchers
- sieve
- 5 glasses
- hot water
- test substances: vinegar, lemon juice, antacid liquid, baking soda

1 Tear the red cabbage into small pieces, and put them into one of the pitchers.

2 Pour in enough hot water to cover the cabbage. Let it stand for about 30 minutes.

3 Strain the cabbage juice into the other pitcher.

4 Pour the cabbage juice into five glasses.

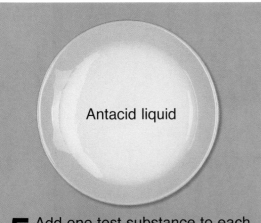

5 Add one test substance to each of the glasses. Compare the results with the cabbage juice.

Antacid liquid

Cabbage juice indicator

Antacid liquid turns it light blue

Baking soda turns it blue

Vinegar turns it dark red

Lemon juice turns it light red

Baking soda

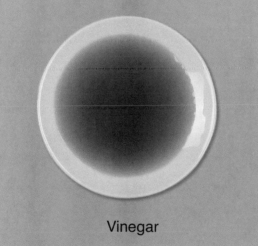

Vinegar

Lemon juice

Acids and alkalis

Acids and alkalis are strong chemicals, but weak forms are found in all sorts of substances. Acids, such as lemon juice and vinegar, turn the cabbage juice a red color. The antacid liquid and baking soda are alkalis, and turn the juice blue. Acids and alkalis cancel each other out when mixed together.

Stinging things

The stings of bees and wasps are both very painful, but for different reasons. Bee stings contain acid, and an alkali such as soap will help ease the pain. Wasp stings contain strong alkalis, so an acid such as vinegar will help stop the stinging.

Bee

Wasp

Magic milk

Make a colorful milk mixture

You will need:

- plate
- milk
- food coloring (different colors)
- liquid soap

1 Pour some milk onto the plate. Make sure it fills to the rim.

2 Add some drops of food coloring to the milk. Use a few different colors if you can.

3 Add a few drops of liquid soap to the center of the mixture.

The liquid soap breaks the surface tension

Pond skaters

The surface tension of water is strong enough to support small insects, such as this pond skater.

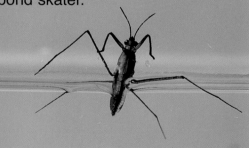

Surface tension

The molecules (the smallest parts) of the milk pull each other together, which stretches the surface of the milk into an invisible skin. This effect is called surface tension. Adding the liquid soap weakens the surface tension and makes the molecules move around. This makes the food coloring mix together.

The milk molecules move apart

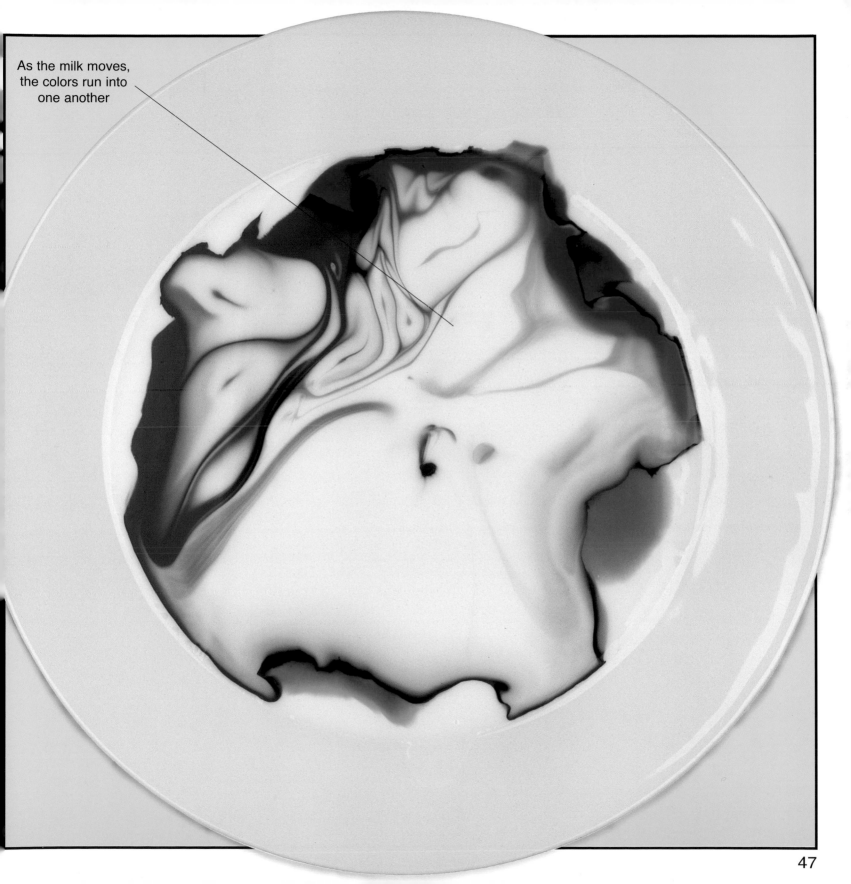

As the milk moves,
the colors run into
one another

47

Giant bubbles

Make huge water bubbles

You will need:

- liquid soap • water
- glycerine or corn syrup
- large bowl (or a large pizza tray if you want to make less mixture)
- wire coat hanger
- skein of string
- electrical tape • pitcher

About bubble mixture

To make really good bubbles, for every 15 parts of water, mix in one part of liquid soap and a quarter part of glycerine. You can buy glycerine from drug stores, but it is quite expensive, so if you plan to make lots of bubbles, corn syrup is a good, cheaper substitute.

Bubble mixture can be kept for several days. Give it a stir before each use

1 Mix the liquid soup and the glycerine in a pitcher. Stir it into a bowl full of water.

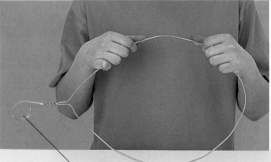

You may need an adult's help to bend the hook

2 Bend the wire coat hanger into a round shape. Bend in the hook so that it is closed up.

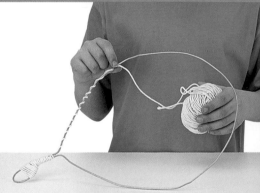

3 Wind string tightly around the hook, and then coil it around the rest of the coat hanger.

4 Secure the string by wrapping electrical tape around the hook. You now have a bubble wand.

5 Dip the bubble wand into the bowl. Make sure that all of the string is covered with the mixture.

6 Remove the bubble wand and let some of the mixture drip off.

Can you keep the bubble wand moving to make a long sausage shape?

Twist the bubble wand sharply to make a free-floating bubble

7 Make bubbles by moving the bubble wand through the air. How big can you make them?

Stretchy water

Water molecules hold themselves together by surface tension. Liquid soup weakens the surface tension, allowing water to be stretched into thin film. A free-floating bubble filled with air will always form a sphere. This is because the surface tension is pulling it back into shape, just like a rubber balloon.

Magnet test

Experiment with magnetism

You will need:

- 2 bar magnets
- horseshoe magnet
- objects to test such as:
  plastic spoon,
  coins, tinfoil,
  pencil, paper clip

Magnet magic

All magnets have two ends with opposite forces to one another. These are called the north and south poles. The opposite poles of two magnets will attract each other. The same poles will repel (push each other way). Magnets attract things that are made of, or contain, iron or steel.

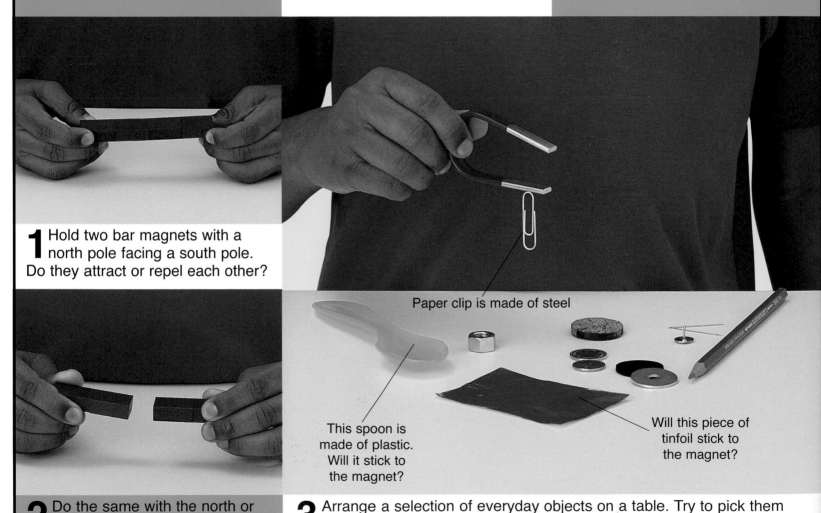

1 Hold two bar magnets with a north pole facing a south pole. Do they attract or repel each other?

Paper clip is made of steel

This spoon is made of plastic. Will it stick to the magnet?

Will this piece of tinfoil stick to the magnet?

2 Do the same with the north or south poles facing each other. What happens?

3 Arrange a selection of everyday objects on a table. Try to pick them up with your magnet. Which ones are attracted to the magnet? Which ones does it not pick up?

Floating compass

Find North with a needle

You will need:

- magnet
- sewing needle
- piece of cardstock
- tape
- plate or bowl
- water
- compass
- scissors

1 Cut out a circle of cardstock about 2 inches across. Tape the needle along the middle.

2 Stroke the needle with the magnet about 20 times in the same direction.

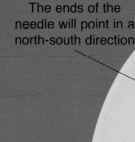

The ends of the needle will point in a north-south direction

3 Fill the plate or bowl with water and float the cardstock and needle on top. What happens?

Use the compass to check the direction of your floating needle

Pole pointer

The magnetized needle, like all magnets, has a north and south pole. These line up with the Earth's North and South poles.

Balloon power

Explore static electricity

You will need:

- balloons
- sweater or t-shirt
- a friend
- tissue paper

1 For all of these experiments, 'charge' the balloons by rubbing them against your t-shirt or sweater.

Balloons stick to your t-shirt

2 Charge a few balloons. Can you make them stick to yourself or a friend?

Hair is attracted to the charged balloon

3 Try holding a charged balloon over a friend's hair. Can you make it stick to the balloon? This works best if your friend has long, fine hair.

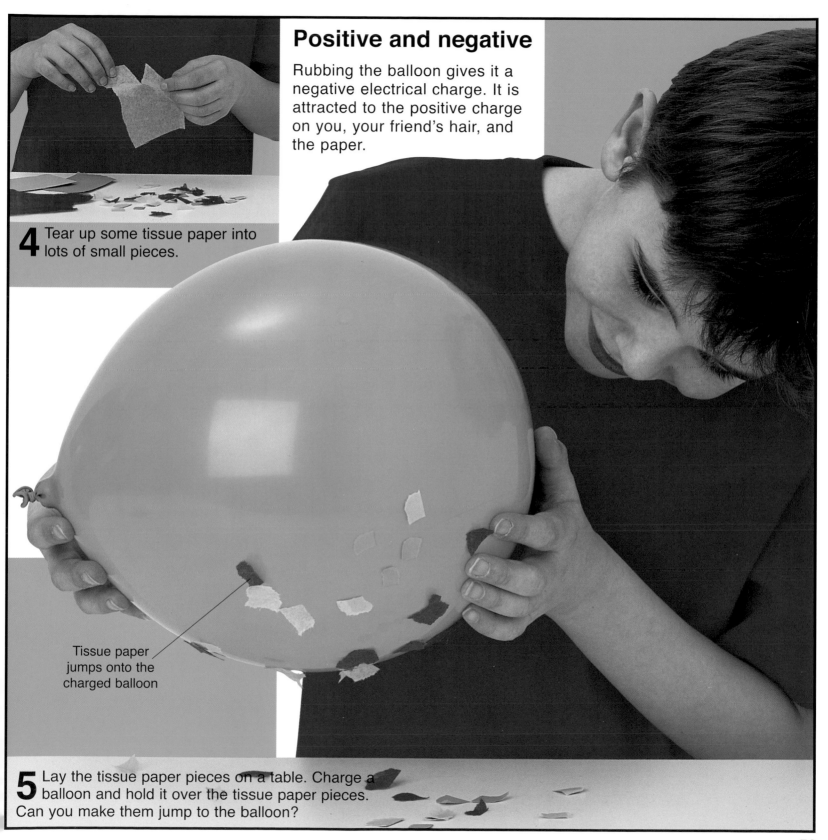

Positive and negative

Rubbing the balloon gives it a negative electrical charge. It is attracted to the positive charge on you, your friend's hair, and the paper.

4 Tear up some tissue paper into lots of small pieces.

Tissue paper jumps onto the charged balloon

5 Lay the tissue paper pieces on a table. Charge a balloon and hold it over the tissue paper pieces. Can you make them jump to the balloon?

Balloon power

Move things with a balloon

You will need:

- balloons
- sweater or t-shirt
- empty soda can
- faucet

Moving particles

Everything is made of atoms, which contain tiny particles called protons and electrons. Protons are always positive and electrons are negative. Rubbing the balloon moves electrons onto it, and it becomes negatively charged. The parts of the water and soda can closest to the balloon get a positive charge, and are attracted to it.

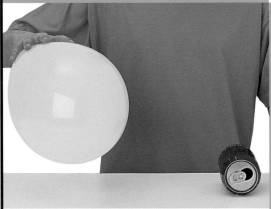

1 Put the can on a table on its side. Hold a charged balloon about 12 inches away from it.

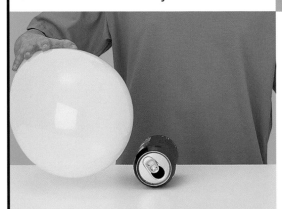

2 Can you make the can roll towards the balloon?

The uncharged balloon has no effect on the water

3 Turn on a faucet to get a very fine stream of water. Hold an uncharged balloon near it.

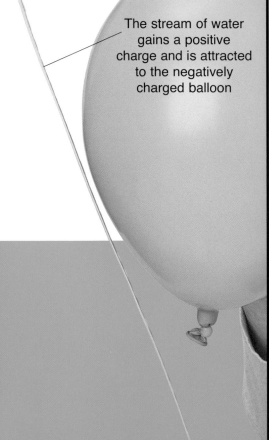

The stream of water gains a positive charge and is attracted to the negatively charged balloon

4 Now do the same with a charged balloon. What happens?

Radio waves

Transmit a radio signal

You will need:

- battery
- 2 pieces of wire with exposed ends
- electrical tape
- portable AM/FM radio

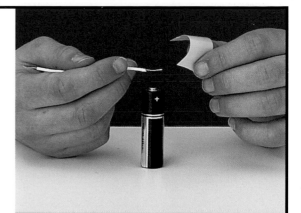

1 Attach a piece of wire to one of the battery contacts with a piece of electrical tape.

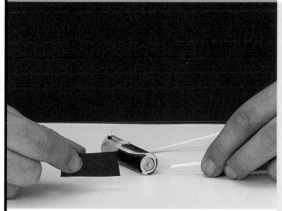

2 Attach the second piece of wire to the other contact.

3 Touch the two free ends of the wires together. You should see a tiny spark.

The radio picks up the signal as a crackling noise. This is created by the battery's electrical current

Spark signals

Radio signals are produced by electrical currents, which travel through the air in waves. You have made a tiny radio transmitter that sends its own radio signal when you make the spark.

Touching the wires together creates...

4 Switch on the radio and select the AM band. Tune it so that it is not receiving any station. Hold the battery a few inches away from the radio and touch the wires together. What can you hear?

Pretty flowers

Make a white flower colored

You will need:

- white flowers (carnations are best)
- tall glasses
- scissors
- water
- food coloring (at least two different colors)

2 Cut the stems of the flowers about 4 inches from the end.

4 Take another flower and split the stem up towards the flower head.

1 Fill three glasses about two-thirds full of water. Add some food coloring to each glass.

3 Put one flower in each of the glasses and leave them somewhere to stand overnight.

5 Put one half of the split stem in one colored water glass and the other half in a different color.

Red

Yellow

Red and white

Red and blue

Standing a flower in two colors makes a multicolored flower head

Deep drinkers

Plants, like all living things, need to drink water to survive. This experiment shows how flowers get their water from the ground. The colored water is sucked up through the stems and into the petals.

Bottle tornado

Make a whirling water vortex

You will need:

- 2 plastic soda bottles
- rubber washer (same size as the bottle opening)
- electrical tape
- water
- food coloring (optional)

1 Fill one of the bottles about two-thirds full of water. Add some food coloring if you wish.

2 Put the washer over the mouth of the filled bottle. Tape it in place, leaving the hole open.

Forces and pressure

The water is held in the top bottle by the air pressure in the lower bottle, and the surface tension of the water in the washer. Spinning the bottle creates a turning force in the water that breaks the surface tension, allowing the water to flow. The air in the lower bottle is then forced into the top.

3 Balance the mouth of the second bottle on top of the washer. Fasten the two bottles together with electrical tape.

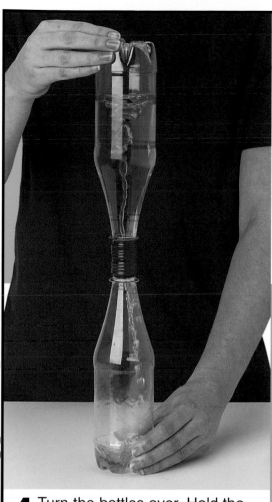

4 Turn the bottles over. Hold the base of the empty bottle, and move the top one in rapid circles.

Water or air moving like this is called a vortex

5 Let go of the bottles, and the water should flow into the bottom.

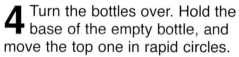

Turning tornadoes

Tornadoes are made by funnels of warm air rising from the ground being made to spin by strong winds. The pressure inside the tornado is much lower than the air around it, which is why they suck things up like a huge vacuum cleaner. Tornadoes can twist at speeds of up to 310 mph.

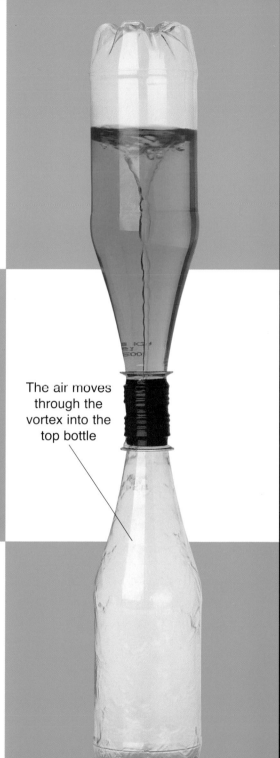

The air moves through the vortex into the top bottle

Rising heat

How does heat move?

You will need:

- 2 plastic soda bottles
- food coloring
- 1 1/2-inch x 1 1/2-inch piece of cardboard
- hot and cold water
- bowl

The hot water rises into the cold water

Some of the cold water sinks into the lower bottle

Do this experiment in a bowl

1 Fill one bottle with cold water, and one with hot. Add some food coloring to the hot water.

2 Place the piece of cardboard on top of the bottle of cold water, and hold it firmly in position.

3 Carefully turn the bottle of cold water upside down, and put it on top of the other bottle.

4 Make sure that the bottles are lined up. Ask an adult to help you take out the piece of cardboard.

Convection currents

Heat always moves from a hot place to a cold place. The hot water molecules are moving around more than the cold water molecules, which means that the hot water expands and moves into the cold water. This movement is called convection. This is how heat moves in all liquids and gases.

Glossary

Words in **bold** are explained in this glossary

Acid

A type of **chemical** that can eat away at substances. Weak acids are found in everyday things such as lemon juice, and have a bitter taste. An **indicator** turns red when mixed with an acid.

Aerodynamic

Something that flies well through the air has an aerodynamic shape. This is because its design reduces the effect of **drag.**

Airfoil

The curved shape of an airplane wing. Its shape creates the **force** of **lift,** which gets the airplane off the ground.

Air pressure

The **force** with which air presses down and pushes against things.

Alkali

The **chemical** opposite of an **acid.** Alkalis **dissolve** in water, and cancel out, or neutralize, the effect of an **acid.** An **indicator** turns blue when mixed with an alkali.

Atom

The smallest part of an **element.** Everything around us, in the world and throughout the universe, is made up of atoms.

Attract

The invisible **force** that pulls **magnets** towards each other. The north **pole** of one **magnet** attracts the south **pole** of another **magnet.**

Balance

A position where something has equal **weight** on either side. The point where something balances is called the center of **gravity.**

Balanced forces

When two opposing **forces** push or pull against or away from each other to keep something in one position. A bridge stays up and supports things because of balanced forces pushing and pulling throughout its structure.

Battery

A source of **electricity. Electric current** is created in batteries by two different materials (usually zinc and another metal) reacting with an **acid.**

Carbon dioxide

A **gas** that is breathed out by people and animals. It is also made by some chemical reactions, such as when baking soda and vinegar mix together.

Chemical

A single, pure substance. It can be changed when it is mixed with another substance.

Chromatography

A way of separating a mixture into its different ingredients by passing it through something. For example, separating out the colors in candies by running them through blotting paper.

Condensation

When a **gas** turns into a **liquid,** usually by cooling down.

Conduction

The movement of heat through a **solid.**

Convection

The movement of heat through a **liquid** or a **gas.**

Density

How tightly packed together the material inside something is, relative to its size. For example, the material inside a small, heavy marble is very tightly packed together – it has a high density. A large, empty box has a low density.

Dissolve

When something breaks up into very small parts in a **liquid.** For example, sugar dissolves easily in water.

Drag

The **force** that slows down an object as it moves through a **liquid** or **gas.** For example, a parachute is slowed down by the drag of the air pushing against it.

Electrical charge

What is produced when an **atom** loses or gains **electrons.** Rubbing a balloon **attracts electrons** to it, giving it a negative charge. If something loses **electrons,** it gains a positive charge.

Electric current

The rate at which **electrical charge** moves.

Electricity

A type of **energy** created by **electrons** moving from one place to another. **Static electricity** occurs naturally, but the electricity we use at home is generated in power stations.

Electron

A **particle** of an **atom** with a negative **electrical charge.**

Element

A substance made up of one kind of **atom.** An element cannot be broken up into something else.

Emulsion

When the droplets of one **liquid** are suspended in another without **dissolving** into it. For example, adding some liquid soap to a glass filled with oil and water makes an emulsion.

Energy

This can be described as the 'ability to do work.' Energy comes in many forms, including light, heat and electrical energy.

Evaporation

When a **liquid** changes into a **gas,** usually when it heats up.

Force

A push or pull. A force can 'do work,' such as speeding things up, slowing them down, or changing their shape.

Gas

A substance that will expand to fill any space that it occupies.

Gravity

The **force** that makes things pull toward each other. Big, heavy things have lots of gravity. The Earth's gravity pulls everything toward its surface.

Indicator

A substance used to test the strength of an **acid** or an **alkali.** Red cabbage juice is an indicator. It changes color according to the strength of the **acid** or **alkali** that is being tested.

Lift

The **force** created by the **airfoil** of an airplane wing. It lifts the airplane up into the air.

Liquid

A substance with loosely arranged **particles,** which allow it to move and spread out.

Magnet

A metal object that can pull iron, or anything containing iron (steel, for example) towards it. It can also **attract** and **repel** other magnets.

Magnetic field

The area around a **magnet** inside which iron is pulled toward it.

Molecule

Two or more **atoms** joined together to create a new **particle** of a substance that can exist on its own.

Particle

Used generally to describe tiny parts of things. **Molecules, atoms** and **electrons** are all called particles.

Pigment

A substance that is added to something to give it color. We see the colors in paints and inks because of the pigments that have been added to them.

Pole

One of the two opposite ends of a **magnet.** They are called north and south poles.

Proton

A particle of an **atom** with a positive **electrical charge.**

Reflection

The way that light bounces off something, such as a mirror.

Refraction

The way that light is bent as it passes from one substance to a different substance, such as from air to water.

Repel

The invisible **force** that pushes the north **pole** of one **magnet** away from the north **pole** of another. South poles also repel each other.

Solid

A substance that keeps its shape.

Static electricity

A type of **electricity** produced when two things rub together.

Surface tension

A **force** that pulls together the **molecules** on the surface of a **liquid.**

Vibration

When something moves backwards and forwards very quickly.

Vortex

A whirling movement in air or water that pulls everything to its middle. For example, a tornado.

Weight

The **force** on an object caused by **gravity** pulling on it.

Index